Laugh You

TEXAS!

That 'TEXAS' DICTIONARY
is on Page 92!

by
Joe James

Rocking *J* Press
P. O. Box 1423
Canyon Lake, Tx. 78130-1423

First printing 1996

**Names, situations, and people de-
picted in this book are fictitious.
Any resemblance to actual persons
or similarity to names of people,
living or dead, is coincidental and
not intentional.**

James, Joe

    Laugh Your Way Across TEXAS!
    ISBN 0-9631584-2-2

Printed In the United States of America

SPECIAL THANKS

Getting out a book like this takes skill--but we tried it anyway. And we had help.

First, all these Texans sashayin' around a great and unusual State. Second all the Yankees (anybody North of Dallas) who come and go with the geese. Some come in the summer just to show they can take the heat--and find bargains like this book.

And most important, we had help and counsel from nice folks like Peggy James, Mark James, Colin James, Michael James, Ian Ruder, and Gerry Law. All native Texans except two and we won't tell which two didn't make it.

Author's Lament

Ah say Ah wuz borned in Texas
Like my Momma and my Paw
So please don't tell nobody
Ah wuz borned in Arkinsaw!

Other Books
By the Author

Kill It Before It Moves
Quiet On The Tee
What It Is, Is Golf
So You Are Taking Up Golf
How To Give Up Golf
What The Hell Is Trumps?
Teacher Wore A Parachute
100 Funniest Golf Limericks
Nothin's Funnier Than Golf In Texas

FOREWORD

Texas is a fun state!

Unlike any other state, yet it has some of all the rest within its borders. You'll find mountains, desert, ocean, pine forests, and just about everything but Hawaii's pineapple groves. And while you read this some guy or gal in the Valley may be settin' out pineapple plants.

Texans are different too, yet a lot of us are from all over the U.S. We just became Texans, and started braggin', as soon as we crossed the border.

On the pages that follow we have tried to pass along a little bit of Texas. Laugh with us, and at us, if you are a visiting Yankee. And if you were born in Texas -- maybe a rare breed nowadays -- you've got some laughs coming too.

Y'all have fun now, you hear!

"I wonder what they mean by that?"

"Git off the stove, Tex! You'll never be at
Home On The Range!"

"The circus ain't comin' this year. Let's run up to Austin and watch the Legislature!"

"Ma'am, we don't give out maps. Texas is
so durn purty visitors just hop in
their cars and drive!"

"You all have the 'Texas Flu'. Youah nose is dry but youah mouth keeps runnin' off."

"We must be entering the famous
Texas Steaked Plains!"

"Back off George! That's not a dead armadillo.
It's San Antonio's Alamodome!"

"We've got some tight turns at the ranch. You
got anything that bends in the middle?"

"That sign back there was Highway 125. Not
the speed limit!"

"Ah know Milwaukee is offerin' you eleven and we can only go five million. But just think, you'd get to stay in Texas!"

"Don't give me any novocaine, Doc! Just have
the nurse sing `The Eyes of Texas!'"

"Ah ain't never seen it this hot
in Texas before!"

"You reckon Junior is old enough to tell him
he wasn't born in Texas?"

"That new man is tough but dumb. He's holdin'
the wrong end of the brandin' iron again!"

"Colonel Travis, why don't we stall 'em until
they build that Alamodome!"

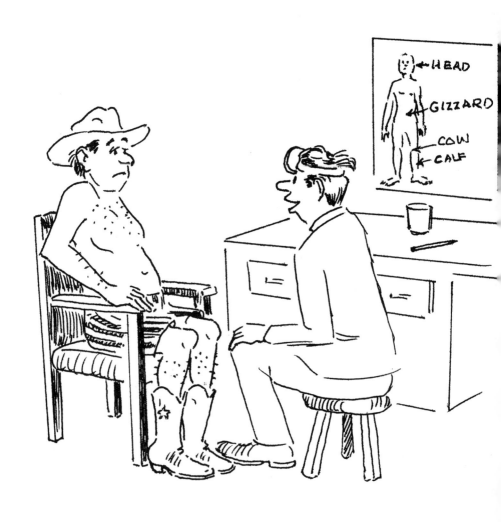

"You got a lot of stuff wrong with you. If you
wasn't a Texan, Ah don't think
you would make it!"

(Mexia is pronounced *Muh-hay-uh*)

"It's my late husband's ticket. I'd give it to a
friend but they are all at the funeral!"

"Ah love goin' into space, but Ah sho'
hate to leave Texas!"

"Gentlemen and Ladies of the Legislature, Ah
recommend we don't put seats on the
Aggie side of the new stadium. They
don't sit down anyway!"

"Sure Ah drive friendly! When Ah cut
somebody off Ah always smile!"

"I don't care if you are the San Antonio Spurs, get those thangs off your feet!"

"We must be in Cut and Shoot Texas!"

"Son, if we didn't throw out trash them people
who adopted this highway wouldn't
have nothing to pick up!"

With a riot threatening, the Mayor wired the
Governor to send a Texas Ranger.

"Dadgummit Marge! You've done gone and got
ouah new Cadillac dirty! You know how
Ah hate to keep buyin' new cars!"

In 1876 Lucas McDonald (no relation to them
other folks), invented the first
Drive-in Chuck Wagon.

"We now have a concealed weapon law in
Texas. You better throw a hoss
blanket over that thang!

"We must be gettin' near Alpine, Texas!"

"At first it was just c-cold but now
it is f-freezing!"

"Stop that! Rattle snakes are protected
in Big Bend National Park!"

"Dadgummit, I'm glad Orville and Wilbur are spared hearin' about this!"

Tails From The Ranch Country

"We ain't payin' our respects to nobody.
We're collecting votes!"

"Son don't nevah ask a man if he wuz born in Texas. If he wuz, he'll tell you.If he wuzn't you'll just embarrass him!"

"We are in Texas now. Better circle the RV's!"

Texas piglets are nice
But they get meaner
When they grow up to be
A Javelina!

Texas road runners
Seldom fly
But they always beep
When they whiz by!

"This must be one of those Texas cattle drives!"

"Ah love this Texas lion dancing!"

"Ah'm lookin' for John Wilkes' booth!"

"This must be the Golf of Mexico!"

"Senor Americano, you will love the thrill of
slipping into your own Country!"

"Don't bother me if you see a tornado.
But holler if you see two!"

"If nobody else wants to say something about
the deceased, Ah would like to say
a few words about Texas!

"Sheriff, they was a flash flood warnin' and
Ah was bein' friendly and movin'
'em to higher ground!"

"Those whooping cranes just discovered they are
a protected species!"

"Don't try to beat down our price. This is
the Chisholm--not the **Chiselin'**--trail!"

"We used to do the cotton pickin' with our cotton pickin' hands but now they do it with a cotton pickin' cotton picker!"

"Ye Gods! I didn't know Niagara Falls was
near New Braunfels!"

"No matter how often they shear me, Ah
keep gettin mo' hair!"

"Us Texans have always made visitors welcome.
Except for that feller Santa Anna!"

"Since all the hotels in Dallas are full maybe we
can rent that John Neely Bryan cabin!"

"That's the Palo Duro Canyon Lighthouse
-- and we've never lost a ship!"

"Of course these are my formal boots. Ah
ain't nevah worn 'em in the cow pen!"

"If they'd built this Bracketville Alamo sooner,
Santa Anna shore would of been confused!"

"We are really in luck! Those are a couple of
rare Texas Box Turtles!"

"Mah Dad used to hang cattle rustlers. Now their lawyers sue us for 'bovine harassment.'"

"Hey, this says there really are bears in Texas!"

"No Senora, we are Mariachis-
not maracas!"

"Don't fight those Texans, General Santa Anna.
Hire some lawyers and write a book!"

"Ah love this State Fair fun house!

"But lady, the river is only three feet deep!"

"Hot damn! We finally got ol' Tex
`Back in the Saddle Agin!'

"They are either bowlers or clumsy carpenters!"

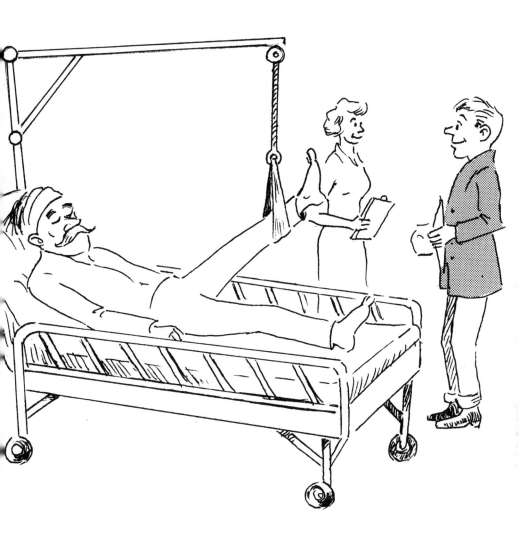

"Mr. Tex was kicked by a horse, but he is
in stable condition!"

"Mah sales have doubled since Ah started
givin' mah hosses false teeth!"

"Remember class! It is Capi-**tol**, not Capi-tal!"

"Twenty eight dollars is too much for lunch--
even if you are in the **recharge** zone!"

"Ouah Texas caverns take you far back
in geologic time!"

"You won't meet any babes photographin'
the Bridges of Loving County. There
is only 170 people!"

"Ah wanted to be a motorcycle officer but
mah hat wouldn't stay on!"

"Tex, youah pickin' is fine but youah grinnin'
needs some more practice!"

We've got it made Sylvia, unless they declare
Texans an endangered species!"

"How much you charge to take this
thang to New Orleans!"

"Mommy, this Ranger Museum sign says `No Smoking'--and he's rollin' a cigarette!"

"We don't have any drive-by shootings in Texas..
Everybody stops and takes dead aim!"

"Fellow Legislators, Texas has a State Flower
and a State Bird. Let's pick us a State
bush--and name it George!"

"The best way to improve ouah Texas legal system would be to dig up Judge Roy Bean!"

"We must be in the Texas <u>Heel</u> Country!"

"That is the only Texan who never bragged about Texas!"

"The Lexington is settin' in concrete. But we
can bust her right out if them furriners
start anything!"

"She has carried a concealed weapon for years.
Her **tongue**!"

"We had to re-do all ouah 'Drive Friendly'
signs after Texas passed the
concealed weapon law!"

"George, you just can't help messin' with Texas!"

A 'TEXAS' DICTIONARY

Ah love to be a Texan
We talk a special way
So all them furrin' Yankees
Won't know what we say!

ABORT-- Plank, e.g.piece of wood
ABLUM--A whole bunch of pitchers
ACIDIFY--Move to the city
ALASKA--Gonna get information
    from a lady.
ALLIGATOR--One who alleges, usually one of them
    lawyers
ALTITUDE--How you feel about somethin'
ABET-- To wager, as in "Abet mah horse can beat yourn"
ADEPT--As in, "After Ah quit smokin' adept snuff"
AFORE--As in, "I got here afore you all."
AH-- First person singular
AGGIE--College student who can afford boots
AMACHOOR--Playin', but not gettin' paid
AMIDE--Likely to do it.
AMBULANCE--Environment, or certain feelin' in a
    room or area.
AMMONA-- As in,"Here's what ammona do!"
ANGLE-- Connects youah foot to youah laig.
AIKEN-- Hurtin' bad.
AIR-- As in,"That air thang"
AIRY-- None, as in "Not airy a one."
AIR PLANE--No doubt about it. "That air plane as the
    nose on yore face"
AMATI--In Yankee land, a fiddle. In Texas, an
    adjective. "He looks amati like his dad."
AORTA-- Subject and verb. "Aorta go feed them cows."
ANTY-CUE-- Anything older'n you.
ASTER--Find out what she knows.

B

BALD--Cried like a baby.
BIDNESS--Anything that makes or loses money.
BANDY ROOSTER--Smaller than big chickens but a
    lot meaner.

BAR--You can belly up to one but not to the furry one.
BARN--How you got here.
BIRL--To heat a liquid til it starts jumpin
BOBBED WAHR--Regular wahr with sharp pointy thangs.
BRAYMER--Bull rider favorite from India.
BRONC-- Horse that knows he is in Texas.
BUCKAROO--A sho' nuff Texan or a Yankee with
                    cowboy boots.
BUGGY--Ain't all there.
BULLIN--Layin' it on purty thick.

C

CHAW--A just right chaw of tobaccy
CHONDER--Way out thar.
CHOW DOWN--Git at the vittles.
CHICKEN RANCH--House where young and old roosters
                    cavorted before they shut 'er down.
COTTON PICKIN'--Used to describe anything except
                    cotton pickin'. We got machines for that.
CHEER-- What you sit on
CHILI-- A bowl of red stuff strangers should tackle
            with caution.
COBEER--Beer on ice.

D

DARTER--Your girl child.
DARK THIRTY--night time
DINNER--Lunch
DINGUS--Sorta like a do-lolly
DOCTOR--To hep yourself medically, Like, "Doctor that
            cut on yore laig"
DONE--Accomplished, as in "I done did it!"
DO-LOLLY--Could be a dingus
DOUBLE OGLY--Whupped with an ugly stick
DRAWERS--Unnerwear

E

EXCAPE--To get away
ENCHILADA--Foreman

FAHR--Anything burnin'
FANGER--One of yore upper digits
FURRIN'--Ain't from Texas.
FRIJOLES--Beans.(Free-hole-eez)

G

GUMMINT--Them folks up in Austn or Washington.
GENUWINE--Real thang.
GIT--Latch on to
GIT FIDDLE--A big fiddle. Sets on the floor and you
          pick that thang with yore fangers.
GIZZARD--Yore mid-section. "Thumpin' gizzard"
          on tother hand means yore heart.

H

HEP--To pitch in and hep out.
HIGH ON THE HOG--Really good vittles.
HIS'N--It ain't her'n
HER'N--It ain't his'n

J

JAWIN'--Chewin' the fat

K

KEERFUL--Like you wuz in rattlesnake country.
KYE-OH-TEE--Coyote.

L

LICK--Whup up on somebody
LIBELLY--Where they keep the books.
LIGHT OUT--To get movin' fast.
LITTLE WOMAN--Youah wife
LIGHT A SHUCK--Hit the road real fast.

MAH--It's mine
'MERCAN--One of our fellow countrymen
MAVERICK--An unbranded calf or stray. Or,a Texan
     who don't always run with the herd.

N
NACHOS--Or dervies with a zip to 'em
NO HOW--Ain't no way.

O
ORTER--You all should do it.

P
PITCHER--Worth a thousand words.
PLUMB--All purpose word."Plumb tired, plumb lucky.
POKE SALAD--"Greens" cooked from young pokeweed
     shoots. (Roots are poison)
PUT THE BIG POT IN THE LITTLE ONE--Throw a really
     wing ding party.
PURTY--Like Texas wimmen.

R
RANCH--Rinse off with water.
RANCH--A handy tool.
RAT--At hand. "It is rat cheer where ah put it!"
RAT CHEER--You know this one. You read it rat cheer.
RETCH--To stretch out for something."Retch me the
     potatoes.

S

SEED--Past tense of saw.
SPITTIN' IMAGE--Handles chawin' tobacco like his
     old man.
SQUOZE--What you shouldn't a done to that pimple.
STEEPLE--Fastens bobbed wahr to a post.
SUPPER--Dinner in Yankee land.
SWOLE--What yore fanger did when you hit it with
     that hammer.

THANG--Any single entity.

TAINT-- Isn't, not true.

TAMALE--Eats good if you take off the corn shuck
        first. (Tuh-mah-lee)

TEA SIP--University of Texas student or Ex.

TORTILLA--Handiest thang they serve with Mexican
        food. (Tor-tee-yah)

TAR--What your car wheel runs on.

TEXAS SPORTS CAR--Pick up.

TUCKERED OUT--Pooped

U

UNNERWEAR-- Drawers

V

VITTLES--What you get at dinner or supper.

W

WHUP--Beat up on somebody that needs it.

WARSH--Scrub with soap and water on the warsh
        board and ranch off.

WRANGLE--Hassle cattle and move 'em along.

Y

Y'ALL--All of you all.

YALLER--As in, "Yaller Rose of Texas"

YOUR'N--It's got your brand on it.

WANT TO HEP? This "Texas" Dictionary ain't near
complete. If you have some words that oughta get
added, send 'em to:
Rocking J Press, Box 1423, Canyon Lake, Texas. 78130